THE GLEANER SONG

Also by Song Lin:

In Chinese
City Dwellers (1987)
Vestibule (2000)
A Visit to Dai on a Snowy Night (2015)
Oral Message (2016)

In Translation
Fragments et chants d'adieu (2006)
Murailles et couchants (2007)
Sunday Sparrows (2020)

SONG LIN

THE GLEANER SONG

SELECTED POEMS

Translated from the Chinese by Dong Li

First published 2021
from the Writing and Society Research Centre
at Western Sydney University
by the Giramondo Publishing Company
PO Box 752
Artarmon NSW 1570 Australia
www.giramondopublishing.com

Designed by Jenny Grigg
Typeset by Andrew Davies
in 9/15 pt Tiempos Regular

Cover image: YVdavyd

Printed and bound by Ligare Book Printers
Distributed in Australia by NewSouth Books

A catalogue record for this book is available from the
National Library of Australia.

ISBN: 978-1-925818-70-3

The Giramondo Publishing Company acknowledges the support of Western Sydney University in the implementation of its book publishing program.

This project has been assisted by the Commonwealth Government through the Australia Council, its arts funding and advisory body.

To my loved ones

&

In memory of the days and nights on the road

Contents

The World Migrating: On Translating Song Lin

Dong Li

I got to know Song Lin well while at Ledig House for a Translation Lab residency. On a long walk in the countryside of Upstate New York, I saw his eyes light up as a deer leapt from the wild into a wide-open field. As the evening hues shifted farther into the forest, his line of sight followed the deer until it vanished into the night. We talked about the deer, and later he asked me to translate a poem that he had written to record the occasion. This is a curious poet who opens himself to the world around him. His songs migrate from one word to another, from one language to another. The landscape of his travels becomes a map of his poetry, which, in turn, amounts to a sensitive anthropology of our migratory world.

Not unlike his predecessor Bei Dao, whose candid declarations of resistance marked the tenor of the time, themes of politics and exile permeate Song's poetic output. When the Tiananmen event exploded in Beijing, Song led student demonstrations in Shanghai and was imprisoned for almost a year. But unlike many self-claimed 'exiled poets', Song has never used imprisonment to his advantage. Instead, what has interested Song is the joy of making art out of words and how poetry can group words and form company. His joy in poetic expression led to his lengthy wanderings through France, Singapore, and Argentina. These heightened his sense of language and its central role in his poetry.

Song has been somewhat neglected in his native language. Political pressure was the unspoken background. During those wandering years, his two formidable titles *Fragments et chants d'adieu* (*Fragments and Farewell Songs*) and *Murailles et couchants* (*City Walls and Sunset*) appeared in French bilingual editions. He was unable to publish in China then, so he used his editorship with the eminent journal *Jintian* to scout out and publish poets living under difficult circumstances. Since his return to China, he continues to support young poets and champions translation. Unlike many poets who are eager to please Western ears, Song advocates for the classics and for a thorough study of the Chinese language. When dividing lines between different camps of poetry and poets widen, Song is the one, not to force cohesion, but to promote tolerance and understanding.

Song's faith in poetry and his generosity towards poets across aesthetic, generational, and national boundaries make him one of the most unusual poets to have emerged in recent Chinese history. His poetry weaves through American, classical Chinese, French, and Latin-American traditions. His influences are the modernists, the surrealists, the romantics, the deep imagists and the objectivists – but what distinguishes Song is his ability to take them all, and make them his own, and make them new. His is a lyric that continues to open up horizons.

1

Like a leper who can never return home,
exiled time throws up its white foam
under the cliff, in the thorns of starlight.

The Gleaner Song

1

Calling out in a partridge's dialect while running out of the house,
I could hear a voice in the blueberries:
radar station, wooden carriage, childhood hillocks
that we had been looking for all summer.
The slopes open and smooth, the urn of the dead
half buried. Bleak words, as if dipped in honey.
Our paradise slanted to the south, the canaries flying about.
There was no Troy then, we always lay down and watched
the village, the tall fir tree, like in *Classics of Mountains and Seas*.
There were axe marks left by the construction workers from
        another town.
'No good end for a trouble-maker,' the elderly said
and we laughed, hiding in the curse, flashing a mirror.

I flicked embers in winter and went to the mountains in summer,
gleaning, sat in the tree waiting for Father.
The bridge disappeared, as if washed away by a summer storm.
This was a place with no beginning nor end.
People just walked around a few fir trees
and lived in their calendars. A fox screeched, a heavy fog
chased after us. A long-distance bus climbed up from the seaside.
Without Father, we kicked broken rocks around and came home.
At night I had a wet dream. Ah, armfuls of berries.

Do you remember? Those two bright syllables
turned us into blue ghosts. Even the wind blued
a wild children's song: 'radar soldier, radar soldier from the sky'
until the moon rose in mid-autumn, the wooden carriage slid,
berries crushed, as if blood from a wound, as if to dye
my manuscripts so they read with that kind of blue.

Note: 'flashing a mirror' is a mythological way of casting light on disguised evil, turning it back to its original shape and killing it with the light. 'Those two bright syllables' refer to the Chinese word for blueberry (蓝莓lánméi).

2

Rue Montorgueil. My son exclaimed: 'blueberry'.
Fresh berries were on the shelves. Lovers kissed and embraced.
Tanned skins emitted a smell of seaweed.
Vacation was already over. The Mediterranean left to the
        grave watchmen.
We avoided beach tents and were drawn by animal tracks
and got lost in the beech forest. I wanted to touch
the siren rock on the high ground but eventually
the urge was false, perhaps she died in an avalanche of snow
like the giant salamander in the tree. And legend lived on the tip of
        the tongue.

We all liked summer in the southern mountains.
Country paths lay vertically by our doorsteps, flowers shaded the balcony.
Those who went for a walk by the lake came back
with freshly picked wild chrysanthemums. Mountain peaks lit one
        by one,
the reservoir tender with feelings, the roof ever softer, the
        lingering clouds
in the water's reflection looked like a washing woman turning around
in the opposite mountains, cattle bells resounded. My son squatted
in the shrubbery, his summer at the age of four, not knowing
the origin of his Chinese name, he ate the word blueberry and looked up
and saw a glider, like a kite, which swiftly passed the waterfalls.

My headache was gone, the dictionary brought in
new trouble. In the earth of our bodily elements
the same plants grew, whose branches were there

for the dead. When we put out the homemade jam that we spread
on the country bread at breakfast, how could we explain
black rice and *cold food*, and the lost rituals of worshipping the gods
of heaven?
A concentrated quietude deepened
into the soft and barely warm earth and served me.
Today we were to climb the mountain but chose another path.

Untitled

on a forsythia
autumn shudders
a stranger walks past the river bank
reminiscence turns him into a ghost
towering autumn, a gust of wind
tosses leaf-gold into the garret
your evening battles with a certain angel
until stars become bones

the clock of day naked
a belated meeting beckons
so you cross the square
blue of pine trees around ancient pagodas
no written on the water:
modesty glows on the face of stone
lichen in pain
wordless tongue

Forgetting

1

The sundial   heads   that receded in secret.
Whose meter drew out their false curves?
The altar of your eyes was sunken,
facing an immense building of tomorrow.

When a comet hit Muxidi.
If I were you, you could be him: a mantissa,
her last glance crossed
the bellowing of the deer.

Note: Muxidi was an important access point into central Beijing from the west suburbs. On 4 June 1989 the greatest number of casualties occurred here.

2

The red homonym of snow, spewing
flowers, blooming painlessly.
A flower triggered the opening non-flower of death
which was real. It climbed onto your name

under shrubs in spasm –
prop-like toes were painted in the black salt of fireflies
and were carried away like this,
very much like the scenes of the recent earthquake.

3

Lightning-fast flames from the machine guns
kissed every tender face. The morning taps
washed over and over night's ashes.
The scabs would turn into stalagmites, in the heart.

A missing person came by, a person missing
for too long, his thin arms looking like Don Quixote's.
Countdown time was up. Please read, read like the second hand of
　　the clock
in the rattling of tracks, what has been mired in enmity for a
　　thousand years?

Jiaocheng, 1970

The strait in anguish. Severe typhoons repeatedly made landfall.
The loudspeaker replaced the moon, preaching to the sky the philosophy
    of war.
The longan trees, like the blind, stood on the low hillocks,
nothing to look forward to. The crabs blew bubbles,
still living in their prehistoric recklessness.
The cabins of the boat people leaned against dark shoals.

I was eleven, my face a country moth,
dirty-blonde hair, matted. On a golden shell-case that I found,
I played the national anthem and the Red Youngsters song.
I remember people streaming to watch executions in the suburb.
Like a flood, the crowd stamped on each other, wild with joy
as if running for life, more frantic than during air-defence exercises.

I remember those summer nights, endless street wanderings.
Someone accused me (of course to my parents)
of sneaking into the People's Theatre over the wall to see a model opera
without buying a ticket! Adults splashed water to cool down summer heat;
children were learning how to 'ride a plane' in the alleyways.
I had no evidence but I knew,
among my parents' comrades, there must have been an informer.

He wore sneakers, like a robust athletics teacher.
He stared at me, came closer, his fingernail flicked: faster than
    a grasshopper,
he flicked the melancholy pimple on my forehead.

Q & A

for Fei Yingxiao

1

So, dear lady, once we ask why,
procrastination turns to questioning,
like a sword shrieking in the scabbard, though
the sword carrier is not yet born. So far,
poetry has not surpassed that shrill sound.

2

We are but meteors. The origins
sleep still, waiting to be questioned, but years are quickly gone.
When a line of words loses itself in fog, the dead in us
always return in time, rebutting in anger
or with a smile marking out the path.

3

Writing is a door that opens to the open field,
we come in and out as the sun rises and sets,
there is a trance, difficult to arrive at. So autumn walks here,
paints its inside and deepens itself,
then vanishes, like the glimpse of a red panda.

4

These are differences: the past means to repeat,
the future is difficult to predict; face to face, we
sink into oceanic silence. Close to the bodily edge, wind
rolls. Wind shakes us, like shaking the sail,
and in no time the crossing is done.

5

So we must watch out for the nameless,
for the long lost, for those who belong to greater traditions
that move at a farther place, who are covered in light –
truth, accurate as glass,
is suddenly handed to us.

from **Fragments and Farewell Songs**

A field of emptiness. An anthropological pottery is shattered, impossible to return to its early roundness. The sorrow of wills passes into the next generation.

Crushed by memory, you survive, heart heavy. Fog rises, fog in red, fog on the sea. Like the title deed of a landless owner is the passport that you now clutch in vain. The suitcase is your canoe, creaking through the crowd. Sweat on the forehead. Taste of salt in mouth corners. Black shrubs blossom on barbed wires. You are the lucky one who recognises one of the flowers. The suspicious light of borders flashes on your face. An enmity. When the hand retreats from the small opening of a window, the systematic burn of the stamp scars the skin. Are you ready to leave, you the prisoner? A few brittle reams of manuscripts, the will of clouds adrift, the amulet of the family.

Retreating autumn deepens in the city. Water turns from silver to maroon. A fisherman smokes on the bank, looking at the rising tide. The dark tones in the landscape are often overlooked. The bank, grey in the fog. The early-lit lamps drag hidden adventures ahead of their time. In the eyes of a lonely wanderer, the tango outside the cemetery swings to a skeletal dance of death. The puppeteer wears the flashy clothes of a clown: happiness is his red nose and innocence, his poverty. Fog crosses the bridge like a crouching cat. A pedestrian stops to wipe his glasses as if he wants to wipe out his sudden guilt for things long past. You have not changed, except for your ways of looking – the eyes are still stubbornly in love with the world.

Stars and mother tongues, cold auras
fly low in the blood of a stranger.
Like ancient walkers who go to the mountains
and believe in the magic exorcism of amulets, you believe
that the gentian of the roots of words has not died.
On the hard surface of things
an immortal longing takes place – hidden in famous mountains
or sinking in deep wells, oracles as well as bamboo and silk scripts
reveal themselves again, with time,
clay and scratches on the body.
The spirit of the tweezers becomes more and more slender.
Dust blown away. This is the first Heavenly Question:
did the writer of *I Ching* have worldly worries?
The master counted the yarrows and applied them
to the wounds. Thus thousands of years are gone.
Words break on the baked
brittle tongue – as rivers
come together before the emergence
of that vast stillness, lying forgotten under the slagheaps.
Wherever you are, the pale fire of mother tongues
lights through sleep and is with you
as you get closer to an iceberg in the tundra.
When the south-pointing chariot turns, Cangjie flies over.

Note: Cangjie is claimed to be the inventor of Chinese characters.

The ninety-year-old grandmother sits, elbows on the tablecloth. Outside the window the sea dims, heavier than lead. Light flees. Massive waves almost press on the roof. Then you think, poetry won't replace bread or build an amusement park over a garbage dump. Oil stains can only be wiped out, bit by bit. You go out, towards a fragment of the ancient city wall.

Always something brimming in the eyes of animals reminds one of nostalgia, a language independent of any voice. The river, facedown, a coolness fills my lungs. In order to drink, one has to kneel forward. I used to kneel down like this in the mountains of home.

> In the reflection a trembling face watches you
> and breaks as you dip your hand in the water
> but you feel it, the feeling stronger than ever.
> Memory is another kind of rage.

This is a letter from elsewhere,
like graffiti around the corner
left by an anonymous alien,
now telling an unknown story.
If the urn of memory
is buried in an unknown place,
how will you tell your own story?
'Father, I have been waiting for your return,
I have been standing on the mountain of our early years,
waiting for you.' As always,
an emptiness hits the spine after an ending.
To take fire out of snow, to walk without a trace,
that is difficult, let alone a life laid down in sacrifice.

from **Death and Praise**

6

these noble deer in the museum
whose shadows reflect a glassware world
stay motionless as the fugue marches on
as faintly the deer, antlers forward,

tread into the infinite warm night of the forest
their secret dance reveals itself to a wolf pack
skin thin like twilight
blood downy, bobbing yet motionless

as the motorcade follows blue fire to find a god
the setting sun scorches the deer-hunters' stretched arms
the deer turn around in a pose that cancels itself

food still fresh in time can only be consumed by time
the deer that fainted twice are now more than excited
and blow the winds of joy out from skeletal caves

17

alas! mottled light of the void – alas! angels
I call you so, day after day
en route to the forest, I see a leopard lurk in you
dissolve and restore itself, not a true being

occasionally it breaks free, entirely at ease
and growls in your deep coma –
the leopard afflicted by burning passion
now faints, without a tease

not only is there a leopard around you
– by the bench, between the arms, in your hair
in each pupil there is also a cub

which tears ruthlessly – when desire returns to your body
and flees with beautiful wounds, you fly over
flinging me onto the leopards, flock after flock –

Paul Celan by the Seine

This unavoidable speechlessness: alone, in a foreign land. Alas, 'winter warms us'. This impossible supineness: a dead man floats over the Seine.

Paul Celan drinks the Seine to his heart's content. The more he drinks, the thirstier he becomes. From partial darkness to the full: he drinks away the root of the last word.

The purest go for death the earliest. Resistance off the map – you, glorious deserter, abandoned the concentration camp, the youth, the laughable Nazis. You returned shame to the witnesses, were exiled still, beaten, sought salvation.

Afloat, from the Seine to Jordan, from Paris to Jerusalem. Paul Celan drinks with his eyes, drinks in his own inventive ways. Alone, he drinks the two rivers from heaven and hell.

His eyes open in our eyes. 'When god asks me to drink,' he says.

Note: the line 'The more he drinks, the thirstier he becomes.' is adapted from Arthur Schopenhauer.

Max Ernst

he gave people the knowledge to fight terror
a power station generates electricity in a bird's belly
night shines brilliantly

ten thousand birds fence off darkness beyond the cordon
the plants' weddings more lavish than ever
yet humans are not invited
they cross the river in the slumber of shame

A Walk Down Montmartre

Fog feels like a fever. Under neon lights
a stumbling drunkard holds an electric post
as if holding an angel, pouring out his heart.
I walk down the grey hill of Montmartre.

The windmill of Moulin Rouge slants on the Paris sky,
beer glasses brim with foam. By night's edge,
a cat dreams of a Daliesque painting:
the moon sniffs at strawberries and cream on the serving plate.

The carnivalistic fatal swing of the flesh.
Whirlwinds of saxophone and Tarantella sisters,
crystal shoes on a spell endlessly spin.
There in the telephone booth, a lady cries out.

After a sad expatriate party,
I want to sleep! Let absinthe, this green gloomy spirit,
escort me till the end of a night adrift, a drenched night.
I walk down the grey hill of Montmartre.

Tell me, old man gleaning in the trash,
on which street, around which glittering corner,
do I see you again, a figure from the verse of Baudelaire,
whose empty glance would destroy the world?

Bois de Boulogne

scattered lake's silver, west of Paris
Leo jumps through a fire hoop

pine needles, your ritual props

wind fingers your greying hair
eyelashes, wild grass of unkempt shadows

an oar, a silent arm that slices the sky
draws out loops, arid like a sandwell dug up by children
now falling apart by the dream shore
breath intersects wind
clusters of water droplets in the pine-forest twilight
hang onto the garret of a recluse

a giant's head, no one accepts
the old clock far on the Île de la Cité varnishes the ferry
and unlocks the memory of death-row inmates

dear flamingo, the lyre that you pine for
plucks the lake's heart
in the rainbow, blind gold is blown away
Good Friday of raspberries
Wood Demon appears in the circus
I Ching's six-line statements of bitter sour plums
no date of return

from water loop to water loop
crown of stars smashed by the night witch

from under the iron tower a fugitive arrives

The Circus

1

a sly cloud before the eyes
mimics a horsewoman's red hair
or how a sneaky person
reacts upon seeing it

2

whistle a little tune
cut through a beauty, dismember her
take out stiff flesh from silk
no blood drips, no fear
an earth angel, coloured wings on fire
fights with herself, saving herself on the hop
everybody is on the hop saving himself
roles change in no time

3

acrobatics. wind. a hat spins
and drops on the ground, he has to bend

4

a sword pierces through a throat
a sword in suspense
too much attention smashes it to dust

5

swing, rise, time to show off on the bar he realises
human is but a kind of ape and you? if you are an angel
do you always watch from the vault and say sorrow is craft

6

diffuse night, degree zero
the sperm whale of words returns to the seabed
now he is an island, lonesome
phenomenology on the steel cable
he is his own partner in crime
dart and board
a god named Ulysses
nose ice-cold

7

on the bike
ten people make themselves into a wall
muscles rhyme and tower into clouds
ten people turn themselves into a peacock
spin and hold on
as if they made it –
into a naked peacock

8

fire blown towards the audience
lights up the void
becomes one with the stars
or as still as if a meteor had rolled onto a carpet

9

this is craft, wings of poetry
a sport that surpasses
no physique or its clumsiness
in their extreme effort they mirror each other
poetry and a person's frog jump
no trespassing the distance of surprise

when the angel's swing swings by

10

she calls the herd of horses the rippling time
whip, shoo, roll call
a round after a round, glittering
among them she resembles a dignified queen
though she could never tame
that hybrid that absurd
last centaur

Near

Homesick of wine. A song. Ennui, anguished reminiscence. What separates me from the faraway? Looking back on a whim, is it a mirage of the way home that wavers in the mind? Crane, the ice that flies through the void.

Should our homeland be not barbaric, there would be no more wanderers. This dim weather, unknown to us, inherits sorrows from long-gone forevers. The past is the future. In the noise of greed, the giant dragon that symbolises our race becomes tamed by ever-greater greed. The unicorn horn, the phoenix crown have long vanished into thin smoke as music and mores crumbled to ashes. The world bloodlessly emerges in the double image of volcano and flood, as ruins expose the beauty of doomsday.

Dear poet, pour your exiled voice into the long-forgotten cranial cavity, not too late, nor too early. 'Liberation,' an ancient blessing for the oppressed. Unless we warm our bones with wine, aren't the days unbearably long when we take tears for food? Wine jumps from the crane's cabin and opens for us a parachute to the groundless void.

From the days, dangling, now nears us, starry sky and terror near. I stand between this break and the next breaking, as if a buoy left on the river by light. Separation, restraint, living is to drink with death.

Metaphor of the Floating Life

On the twelve identical bridges
not a single one without endless streams of traffic.

The evening bell tolled, birds retrieved their shadows,
steeples faded into a grey sky.

Eyes in a daze, last leaves in the wind
kept trembling, not knowing where to fall.

A spurt of feelings from the divided self
as if you stood on every one of the twelve bridges.

Listening to praise songs on the wind
you were in an ocean of raging fire.

Paratroopers of the heavy snow still gathering then,
the moths of the soul chopped open the church's candlelight.

Rising up intensely, they became air and darkness.
The wind cried out on the bridge, whose soul was that?

Become yourself, not the soul of another person,
cold and lonely like stars.

In the bustle of traffic and celebration of the flesh,
become a river, washing away silent sorrows.

What about the saint in the pagoda?
Hollowed eyes saw into the universe.

Drooping wings of the little monster by his feet
covered heaven and hell in a flash.

Floating snow blanketed the land of the wanderers,
tree scars, your own traces, so glaring, and glaring.

2

You break in, you the drifter who carries
the birthmark of death. When you wake,
the mirror reflects a date, reversed.

Jorge Luis Borges Imagines China

A sandglass. A second. Touch of the finest skin.
Jade of joy. An itch. Secrets in books you have read
sans a page number sans a punctuation mark.
Chapter of the sun. Chapter of the moon. Chapter of the sea.
A pantomime script. A palindrome poem by an anonymous
author more beautiful than a chandelier, a rotating brocade.
A lady-in-waiting advising the emperor on Night of Devotion.
A chapter from *Erya* or a hexagram couplet from *I Ching*.
Wounded feet and iron shoes of Yu the Great. Waters rushing.
Shu Hai walks barefoot to measure the world, as prototype of K.
(Kafka knows he will never reach the two poles.)
Two gates to Hangu Pass, on the table sits
the first version of *Tao Te Ching*, ink still wet.
Affluent vacuity. Return of disappearance.
A tear from an ancient mermaid drips into a pearl.
Li Shangyin writes an untitled poem to some Daoist lady.
An Argentinian ant climbs up Mount Tai.
Sailors row in unison on Jianzhen's boat.
Matteo Ricci draws in Zhaoqing's *Map of World's Kingdoms*.
The Great Wall of China seen from a spacecraft.
An ancient coin symbolises round sky square earth.
The sound of snow falling on the Grand Bell of Yongle.
The opulence and decadence of oriental Venice in South-of-Yangtze.
Archaeologists' tweezers. Puppets' pulling strings.
Unheard-of mysterious creatures in *Classics of Mountains and Seas*.
Silence of Terracotta Army. Furnace and sword of the Chinese alchemists.
Before a stele in Japan I read through the palms

of my hands the immortal inscriptions of the Middle Kingdom.
A bronze doorknob in Buenos Aires calls out to
another bronze doorknob in a Shikumen from Shanghai.

Tower of Enchantment

On Mount Guanyin an elder points to a Buddhist temple, saying this is the site of Emperor Yang of Sui's Tower of Enchantment, thus the poem.

in the mirror supine lacquer wares shake unwillingly
laughter and wooing, to please the emperor
music rooms, secret chambers, fling and fake for the wedding night

if one presents gold leaf and a jade beast
to catch a glimpse of the royal boat slow on the Grand Canal
why would fireflies deep in the palace take one aback?

he grows old, the arched bridge of his body brims
with boundless spring waters of desire
he drains himself dry, in the loins of the opulent empire

he's anxious to take the whole world into his lattice window
yet fears that his days are numbered and the corridor too short
the beauty of butterfly flowers captivates with killing charm

the mirror spits out assassins who fill up the fields
what he fears after all is himself, in some reincarnation
neck into a brocade band, soberly at a loss

The Sun and Rain of West Lake

The Buddhist relics in the stupa shine at night. During the day
they read the inscription: the ferryman is opening a gate of water!
The once-forbidden inner lake now leaks spring light
with the gift of a brief afternoon play of sun and rain.

From the rippling middle blows the homesick song of silkworms
        and moths –
the sun spits threads in the clouds and weaves nets on the water.
I fish the red carp in your eyes –
come ashore to hold fast this dazzling word.

The lake poets sit and drink up rainbows in the glass.
When wind smokes wave after wave of visitors to sleep,
Su Xiaoxiao comes out of the grave and sings:
where the clouds break, ecstasy after the rain, sigh for the late sun.

Twilight grinds West Lake into the most dazzling word,
lilacs whisper in your tresses, whispering,
the stream of fish in your eyes swims into my arms.
I take out a letter, I rise to the solitary summit to watch you –

like Zhu Yingtai, the willows by the bank put back on their
        maiden clothes
and in a wedding dress of blue smoke, drift to night.
Your lotus heart grows on the water, you reincarnate as a woman
and take me through every pavilion and every secret quarter.

Note: Su Xiaoxiao was a legendary courtesan who lived during the Southern and Northern Dynasties and was buried by the West Lake. Zhu Yingtai is the female lead of a Chinese legend of a tragic love story called *The Butterfly Lovers* 《梁祝》.

City Walls and Sunset

for Zhu Zhu

How different it is to roam in our own land,
no need of archeology for the mere knowledge. You and I
walk by the city walls. In the eastern suburb, a pavilion,
a few birds, an afternoon shared together, a reunion.

Pagodas seen beyond lofty galleries, a lady holds in her arms an
    ancient harp,
on the Qinhuai river moored boats fade into the fleeting glories of
    six dynasties.
A window from ninety-nine inner chambers,
sunflames pallidly drive through.

Drizzle, passers-by, I stare at the muddy street,
above a river of bicycles the ventriloquist swallow turns,
the red horse of fog treads softly on the roof of blue tiles,
I muse on the person who named a mountain Purple Gold.

A lake, wavering patterns of its reflection difficult to describe,
naked like poetry, close to zero.
Opposite things mirror each other, drinkers in a conversation,
rivers and mountains burning close to the touch.

I breathe the second moon of the year with all my organs,
I taste Nanjing as if tasting an orange.
Upon my return, wind through clothes, by the city walls in sunset,
I sprint to a plum tree of blossoms in a fresh rain.

Slow Climb to the Summit of Heart

winding, long – behind thick clouds, the light
cascades. the well, crank like an oar, water grunting
thirst sloshed into the throat and eyes of a vast ocean
a poplar stands alone, a ragged road
that has withstood the heavenly

axe, no road, only up and down south and north, wandering
vast loneliness. no rainbow in the sky, only a mirage of shadows
a kerosene lamp lit in the grotto, a pilgrim's body in tatters
the cane of his soul measures this long winding, this journeying

Notes from South Xinjiang

1. The reckless god reads the braille of the desert.
2. One night in Kupa, I received a telegram from Mars: there were traces of water.
3. Dead rivers look like twisted mummies in the gallery of the sky.
4. Language, dust of dust, flies on the long, long road.
5. An oar stands before the boat-shaped coffin. Sailors of the desert sea, tell me, what kind of sail do you dream of?
6. Business caravans head east, and west. The sun bakes eyebrows, beards, and crusty flatbreads.
7. Go. Once you lie down, you run the risk of being air-dried.
8. From one invisible border to another, I count those disappeared countries.
9. A silkworm once dreamed of Rome; or rather, Rome once dreamed of a silkworm.
10. Breeze in the dense forest, homonym of silk and porcelain.
11. The Han princess Liu Xijun – Sappho of Wusun country – was married to a vast and endless homesickness.
12. Under the statue of Kumarajiva, I thought: perhaps his intelligible translation saved Buddhism.
13. On their pilgrimage to Chang'an, the three Buddhist masters walked in the opposite direction to the three wise men.

14. If Emperor Wu of the Han dynasty knew that the Ferghana horse was a horse with a disease, would the history of Ferghana be re-written?
15. The donors depicted on the murals have thin eyebrows.
16. Stupa – navigation system of the desert.
17. What a pity! Gan Ying saw the sea but did not know which one he saw.
18. Petals of the mandala – one five-baht coin after another.
19. The auricle of the crescent rises on the ruins where Xuanzang preached.
20. In the dark labyrinth of the *karez*, flowing water looks for bright vineyards.
21. Migration – from Sanskrit to Charian, Uighur to Chinese; over battlefields and millennia of forgetting, Maitrisimit flies into my vision like a phoenix.
22. Another Uighur *muqam*: alas the *musailaisi* wine, the ice-cold beauty, come quickly and rub out my burning desire for you!
23. In Kashgar, Shen Wei said to me: there are people wherever poplars grow.

Qinghai

a prayer flag rolls around a heap of round stones
every hilltop wears the same crown
there are more hilltops to whose invisible fissures snow recedes
slumber on the train meandering toward Hoh Xil
a bird drops into a bush of sandthorns
Yellow River ripples in bilious light
turns around a big bay and flows into sunset
a few souls carry sheepskin rafters
rustling lanes, night on the other shore

Tengchong

volcanic ashes, dark like the memory of dead souls
that pile up around those mountains
that the Yi people use to build villages
and to bury the dead

snow warmed by aeonic geothermals
cools down canola flowers and bee brains

tourists balloon up to inspect the wounds of the earth
immense pits, edges bright, like one
urn after another formed by giants,
hold their circular voids inside

after an outbreak, afterwards
bleakness has long reigned in this place
seeds taxed, yet no amnesty order
is issued to pangolins

ginkgo trees and misery survive

after a bath in the hot springs
a thunderbolt bursts out singing
and jolts the sky, out of the blue roofs lit

Autumn Whispers

Lesser Khingan meanders, towards Russia
autumn gives me a teaspoonful of honey that I take back
to the woods to hoard in the cornflower's memory –
why does a black bear cub teeter and totter?
Dripping clouds tear at the tent of the autumn circus,
gongs and drums rumble all the way from Wuying to Manchuria.
Dear Quietude, the net you weave could be used as sacrifice.
Dear Oroqens, what has sliced open your fish clothes?
A tiger avoids us and returns to its leafy habitat.
Insect noise crowns it, in the golden sunset palace.
When does the resin cement into blue amber
in the compost, in the conical coal seam
until it glitters around your neck?
Pine needles turn left and right, the hooks of hairy beggar's ticks
ambush a reckless shadow.
The lake gramophone broadcasts a lullaby to a vole
but it does not want to sleep, it peels down the husk and
gnaws on the corn with its sharp teeth like a clumsy happy recluse.
For love, the transparent inner wings of a grasshopper unfold
and beat like rain on the fine veins of a leaf.
I stop, I listen, I cross the spiders' traps
in the woods, the person I want to visit has not yet returned.
Heavy pine cones that hang outside the window grace the branches.
A bronze horse pendant from the Jin dynasty hangs on the door.
I shake the bell, I startle the sika deer,
I scare away a flight of thrushes feasting on magnolia vine berries.

Dear dead moths, like letter after summer letter stuck
on the glass shade that still seems to push inwards.
No one can call back that 'snap' of sacrifice,
that farewell of a 'snap', doesn't it ever hurt?

Remembering Another Journey on the La Plata River Ferry

Wide as Lethe, this body of water can barely be called a river.
Those on the same ferry might not return together.
Heraclitus lamented before as did Confucius,
but the indisputable river claims its own precepts,
as a river is a tongue of the earth.
A few babies crawl in the cabin where the sun shines,
a city resembles a mottled dinosaur from a quick glance,
those standing at the stern appreciate the security.
The dead are named after rivers, one is left to stand on the shore
to watch, stomp to songs and bless with deep grief.
I think of the Yangtze, once a border river like La Plata,
between Zhenjiang and ancient Guazhou, in the consciousness
vast as a body of water, you converse with me
and contemplate, in an attempt to reach the other shore.
Then our lips become joined.

3

The receding world of the moment longs
to be a sentence, to be hidden in a sentence
and asks you to take the sentence along for the trip.

Providence and Prophecy

for Shi Tao

What divine punishment have they endured, these past poets.
Homer begged his bread on the streets, Qu Yuan floated on the water,
Hölderlin lost his words after being hit by Apollo
and his erudite compatriot Nietzsche cried through the voice of
a madman,
'God is dead!' and, as a result, died in madness.
As for Lin Zhao, whose name corresponds to her terrifying destiny,
she calls out still for a Christian snow.

In all nations on this planet earth exile
runs through the history of mankind, and that of the suffering poets
occupies a significant chapter. Some want to erase
the section *crematory* and replace it with *burning sacrifice*,
some pretend to be living in the golden age and believe in secret
their thousand-year posterity, once death knocks on the door
they hide themselves in the aura of fame.

Paris, rain on Thursday – what Vallejo heard
and then said meandered despite others' misunderstanding.
Not far off, Celan flew down to Pont Mirabeau,
his body, light like a little sparrow, as if from a prepared poem,
cut through a mass of froth. We all know
what *sliced through* Haizi was not the train,
but the mysterious number of 1989.

When another poet was taken away from us,
his mourning friends dug up the prophecy in his works,

as if the core of life wraps itself in the shell of words:
a slip of the tongue, a fatal negligence.
However it is right here that a fact has been overlooked:
between death in a foreign town and waiting for execution
the unsaid sacrifice is survival.

Note: Lin Zhao's first name Zhao 昭 means to rehabilitate, prophesying her posthumous rehabilitation. The 刀 in the character is the radical for knife, suggesting her martyrdom. In the first line of the last stanza, 'another poet' refers to the late Chinese poet Zhang Zao 张枣.

The Death of Osip Mandelstam

if he died a peaceful natural death
with painless pure mystery
leaving people not to protest in grief
but to linger in the splendour of his poetry
if the assassins were not a step faster
in whichever clever ways
to strip him of his golden singing voice
then the writing hand of this poem would not tremble
no! his death was declared in haste
in rehashed words
and still casts shadows after half a century
and attests (as Joseph Brodsky said)
to the Laws of Gravity – a black hole
into which all humanity is sucked
and a person disappears under the sun
this is yet not difficult, with time and space
with a system operated by a giant
even steel ribs would bend
let us remember the evil age
on a planet where poets dwell, the hornet's nest
of a clamorous age already roils
the fists of a tyrant rub out cinders
everywhere, a new escape begins anew
yet here was Vladivostok on the horizon
in a concentration camp near Kolyma
people shut the door leaving him on the bed
as everything was leaving him

even pain would soon renounce him
sorrow no longer groped his left ventricle
a fugitive, on the edge of an empire
alone to bear a most bizarre destiny
hands stretched out to touch the imaginary land
unwillingly with mixed feelings
a man without even a handful of dirt in life
would in death
                                        be welcomed by the earth
what to regret? death is no longer a surprise
dear assassins, now shall you become so amicable!
higher up, his constellation watches everything from above
and blows the last flame into his body
to warm his soul that is numb from the cold
even with one last breath his entire being
still sings the vast burning night sky
like before, like a swallow
that sings in the acceleration of flight
the night sky of a winter day in 1938
obscure like the night of Final Judgement
pale light, imperishable light
dripped onto a Moscow window
inside, a lady was already asleep
the tears on her cheeks had not dried
on the table, an unsent letter filled
with small scribbles of despairing love,
'It's me, Nadja. Where are you? So long!'

To Czesław Miłosz

In the years after you left,
the world remains the same,
only planet earth becomes elusive,
tribulation like retribution falls on the dining table
from the sky, the earth, and the sea.
As I reread your poems, your philosophical tone
of an outcast, like a wellspring from Lithuania
that tirelessly nourishes you and through you others,
like how Dao creates water, water wood, wood fire.
And the burning fire, please tell me
can you create a brave new planet?
There will be no secret police or censorship in the head,
no *broken city*, declining village,
those who put down arms and pick up oars,
arms beaming in gusto and grace of kindness,
wander in a serene valley guarded by the soul mountain.

Yes, all the rivers should flow into order and wealth.
But in my homeland they either diminish,
are cut at the waist or die in shame,
like blue iguanas air-dried in the desert.
I do not know whether a rivulet flows through
where you rest, so that you could keep watch
in peace, so that those who travel downstream
could find on the map a leaf, a stone
or the tipped eyelashes of some lady you praised.
Your *pure and generous words* make me believe

in the blessed kingdom you imagined, not a river disappears.
The most magical one – the river Alpheus –
is said to flow into another continent
after disappearing in the ocean.
So does your voice that crosses dark nights
lapping on an unknown shore, resounding lastingly.

Note: written on 29 June 2011 before Czesław Miłosz's centennial, words in italics are quotes from Miłosz.

Farewell to C.D. Wright

writing, a twilight word
lingers on the black keyboard
perhaps after exhausting the remaining years
the fortunate light will eventually pierce
your gloomy heart through airtight capillaries
there another Pleiades already slants westward
seven stars, like seven bonfires
have not died out
imagination, the queen of truth –
as Baudelaire said, would put on
turquoise earrings from Arkansas for you
and be satisfied with its own masterpiece
a blackbird still sings in your trimmed garden
as it delights in the new snow, as
the fictional queen flees
you hide in the shrubbery
and feel happy for the potatoes
that are boiling in the refugees' wok
when the setting sun visits
again on the slope
the nameless dead

Couplets

1

snowy ridges crossed, lavish night sails of the nameless dead
white birches light up candelabras, dawn rifles azalea dreams

2

tolling the bell in my ears, your invented sentences subvert
the mainstream
and flood into the nation's silencer, a gourd

3

an echo of a thing that makes no sound, as a word strangled
by the umbilical cord, in the still of the womb, deafens the ear

4

a red fox sniffs the snow, detours further, not knowing what a word is,
it knows the smell of snow beats by far the chewing gum of human lies

5

suburbs in pieces, as if struck by thunder. three invisible men lurk outside a pedicure shop
out of the blue, out of words – the CCTV goes out of order

6

among the torture gadgets that he displays, a condom (from a raped woman
stripped of her right to give birth) curls like a penis in a plastic bag

7

the thing that distracts me from poetry wears a charming mask
and behind the mask stands the vast namelessness

8

a UFO cloud emits light. with ample signal enough empathy a few shadows
that shake their giant heads will come down and send souls to the earth

9

I see the entrance to the grave, I figure inside it will be
darker and deeper than Dante's Inferno and already overpopulated

10

this bed, big as the North, takes me along adrift, hospitable ghosts
    come out of night
and hush me to sleep by the rush of water, warm as an ice lamp, I
    fall asleep

11

tell me, dear colleagues, you who keep silent forever at public events
have you redeemed the power you deserve from the deserted masses?

12

fear – legacy from the guillotine, is inherited by silence
I hear the family of silence is prospering and day by day takes tears
    for food

13

the circular trick of history: we will grow old, zombies will not,
watch out, after half a century zombies come back to life again

14

walking into an unwelcoming party, as if arrayed in a feast for the gluttons
I need to shoo away the fly, I have no interest in seeing it bow its back

15

dug deeper, the totalitarian mines only lead to collapse
memory black like coal crystals, light leaks from the sieve of your body

16

at twilight, sitting emaciated on the slope. encyclopedia of the sky opens to me:
on every page the nibs blood red, blood red, blood red

17

in the basement of the 9/11 Memorial, thousands of dead faces stare
 at me in unison
as if we were at the bottom of the same boat, facing sunlight and
 a life in peace

18

uncertainty: the phantom of our age
is like the Loch Ness monster that blows bubbles yet never appears

19

a dream: the detected gene map of the dictator, in the confidential
files, written in codes and invisible ink

20

he has learned to etch words on the water's surface. he has learned
 to look us up
with stone-cold eyes. the swaddled fast runner nearly catches up
 with infinity

21

a paddle, across a thousand curtain-walls thrust by hidden reefs
between sharks' teeth and the watch of a lighthouse, ferries the sun

22

to endure the tribulation of a word, until it spits you out
like a hard core that sprouts in a grave

23

a stone does not flit by itself, exposing the shadow crushed under it
unless there is another stone, another fulcrum

24

if you have seen the courtship dance of two grebes on the water
you will understand the synchronicity of the universe

25

the fallen, lifted by our hands, leaking through our fingers, are the sands
that once belonged to the stars and are now seething like tears

From the Paintings by Anselm Kiefer

Yes, this is the true picture of the earth.
Life mimics art – ruins burn
like memory deep in the mind. We are used
to the many catastrophes that are unnatural, moral
or linguistic. On the edge of a volcanic pit
we drink tea, make love, take a life through purgatory,
wind whistles the gentle blessing of death.
Too much forbearance, when an urban management officer
beats a street vendor; or when a middle school student
is humiliated by her peers, bystanders see her only as a defeated cricket.
Morality slides towards the abyss and the stock market crashes.
Sodium cyanide explodes in another Hiroshima
in the sultry August before the Military Parade is about to begin,
as if the warlord is suddenly awake.
The power of shockwaves all-powerful, (as we saw
in the nuclear war videos of the Cultural Revolution),
in the blink of an eye, the tongue of the fire-spitting monstress
licks through the exhausted dreams of residential building windows.
Beautiful like a liquid being, silver-grey metal flows
and winds forward to swallow the firefighters' flesh.
One among them, who has just tasted the honey of marriage,
soon turns into brilliant rains of fire.
Yes, life mimics art, yet, in its clumsy way,
the signature of ruins remains: a mess.
Skeletons of burned cars
form a terracotta phalanx, massive and mighty,
awaited is the review. Meanwhile the little parachutes of dandelions

drift to the sea with the names of the disappeared.
The workers' sheds are nowhere to be found.
A radio repeats:
tomorrow, *my dear mother will find my bones.*
Can we really stand until dawn?
In fact, an anonymous man points out to us
a secret route out,
would there be no defence on the way?
Authorities are burying the rumours, madmen are writing praise songs,
the truth that we will never know sleeps and snores in the dark.
A girl by the window has her mouth wide open, shocked
by the magnificent mushroom clouds, as if a Sulamith before
    the crematorium.

A Brief History of Language

not a name not a line of sight, never a thorough run of water
– slumbers of the turquoise icebergs. a severe wintry engraver
dances still a transparent dance of death on the transparent
    coffin surface.

arrival of language at that soft slope, after yesterday's mammoths left.
there comes a man in a birch-bark coat, wearing a Dantesque pale face
as if returning from the netherworld. slowly he blurts a word out
    – 'flower'.

A Walk in Upstate New York Country

for Dong Li

The maples are burning and in a few days will dim
and die out in the snow that is embraced by every hill
from near and far, but late autumn will stay longer than I will.
It does not have to scurry on its journey, or return
to a blind and frantic nation.
I come at the right time, with the cunning and curiosity of an
oriental man.
Evening hues colour my eyes with their hospitality
and open them to landscapes unlike this one.
The weather magnifies my good mood three times more.
Some houses sit atop the hill with a farther outlook,
others scatter in the woods or by the road,
fenced up according to custom and social status.
Notices of private property lead me to make a detour.
I am alert but even more so I am envious of the deer herd.
A gentle kick of their hind legs, and they are free to wander in the area
or take the opportunity to study the odd behaviours of mankind.
The loudspeakers of the valley play no music but stillness.
In a sky busy as Broadway, from time to time a private jet flits past
as if a burning match runs through the living and disappears behind
the kitchen.
The little pond suddenly turns smoggy.
Shrubberies lean on grasses. Like witches,
a flight of crows descends softly and exchanges their new mantras
in secret.
(This time around, I do not care how much they scream.)
The sky darkening, headlights of cars flash and seem to ask:

are you lost? Do you need a ride?
No, thank you, I am just walking a little further
to stretch the distance from the old I before the shaking desk.
But the wild geese have no such thoughts.
Neck forward, they fly close to the treetops and their wings,
like the oars of a dragon boat paddler, beat evenly up and down.
They drop their greetings and I politely answer them.
In the wave of a hand, their V-formations are singing across
the full moon.

Acknowledgements

Gratitude to a PEN/Heim grant and a joint-residency at Ledig House. Our sincere thanks to Ivor, Nick, Lisa, Jenny, Aleesha and the whole Giramondo team. Many thanks to the editors of the magazines in which these translations first appeared:

Arkansas International: 'A Walk Down Montmartre', 'Autumn Whispers'; *Asia Literary Review*: 'Forgetting', 'Jiaocheng, 1970', 'The Sun and Rain of West Lake', 'Notes from South Xinjiang'; *Asymptote*: 'untitled'; *Bennington Review:* 'Remembering Another Journey on the La Plata River Ferry'; *Blackbird*: 'Providence and Prophecy', 'The Death of Osip Mandelstam', 'Tower of Enchantment'; *Brooklyn Rail*: '*from* Death and Praise', 'The Circus', 'Couplets'; *Gulf Coast*: '*from* Fragments and Farewell Songs'; *Kenyon Review:* 'Farewell to C.D. Wright'; *Lana Turner:* 'The Gleaner Song', 'Max Ernst', 'Jorge Luis Borges Imagines China'; *Michigan Quarterly Review:* 'Bois de Boulogne', 'To Czesław Miłosz'; *PEN America:* 'Paul Celan by the Seine', 'Near', 'Metaphor of the Floating Life', 'City Walls and Sunset', 'Slow Climb to the Summit of Heart', 'A Brief History of Language' with Translator's Note; *Pathlight:* 'Q&A', 'From the Paintings by Anselm Kiefer', 'A Walk in Upstate New York Country'; *Plume:* 'Qinghai', 'Tengchong'.

About the author and translator

Song Lin's poetry collections in Chinese include *City Dwellers* (1987), *Vestibule* (2000), *A Visit to Dai on a Snowy Night* (2015), *Oral Message* (2016). Two previously translated collections *Fragments and Farewell Songs* and *City Walls and Sunset* were published bilingually in France. He is the poetry editor of the journal *Jintian [Today]*. Among his honours are fellowships from the Nederlands, Romania, and Hong Kong as well as the Shanghai, Dong Dang Zi, Chang Yao Literature Prizes. He has held residencies at OMI Ledig House Translation Lab and Vermont Studio Center.

Dong Li is a multilingual author who translates from Chinese, English, French and German. He is the translator of *The Wild Great Wall* (Phoneme Media, 2018) by the poet Zhu Zhu, the co-translator (with Lea Schneider) of *Gesellschaft für Flugversuche* (Carl Hanser Verlag, 2019) by the poet Zang Di and the Chinese translator of 《相伴》 *Be With* (East China Normal University Press, 2021) by the American poet Forrest Gander. He has received fellowships from Akademie Schloss Solitude, Camargo and Humboldt Foundations, and Yaddo, and support from a PEN/Heim Translation Grant, Ledig House, Henry Luce Foundation/ Vermont Studio Center, and The American Literary Translators Association.